SEVEN SEAS AND UNCOUNTABLE STARS

Translated by

DR Harikrishnan M

TITLE : SEVEN SEAS AND UNCOUNTABLE STARS

AUTHOR: DR HARIKRISHNAN M

Krishnapriya, Palayamkunnu P.O

Trivandrum, Kerala

India

Publisher: Self Published

Edition 1

First Published 2021

ISBN: **978-93-5473-279-9**

Printed at Confidence Press, Thycaud, Trivandrum. Kerala

Contents

From the Poet

This collection of translated poems by Dr. Harikrishnan M reveals to you another dimension of enjoyment of my poetry. I enjoyed so much from; what I could have experienced as every joyful reader would, when I read the English translation of my collection of poems, Seven Seas and Uncountable Stars.

Since poetry exists only on the surface of language, depth is the transcendence of language. Therefore, it can be said that the language of poetry is also an abstract structure of the crust. The language of translation is marked in many places as inadequate for transliteration as thought of commonly but for me poetry is about confronting an abstract system that is different from language.

Dr. Harikrishnan's beautiful translation language has given a new lease of life to this collection. These poems can be taken to greater heights as they are translated into English. It is also a place where one can explore more areas by beautifully combining the languages of poetry and art.

Dr. Rajeev Puliyoor

About the sculptor N N Rimzon

The artist is keen on directing the viewers to a complex experience of his imagining. Inspired by Ram artist Kinker Baij and by German realism and expressionist figuration, N. N. Rimzon likes to exaggerate and then distorts his figures. This artist from Kerala studied sculpture at the College of Fine Arts, Trivandrum and later completed his post-graduation from Baroda's M.S. University. He also went to the Royal College of Art in London after receiving an Inlaks scholarship.

His sculptures are noted for their arrangement in an installation-like space, and are greatly energized by marked contradictions of color, size and varied settings. He has had site specific installations, like 'Far Away from 108 Feet' (1995), which calls for the viewer's familiarity with Hindu social codes and effectively portrays the survival of the caste-system in India; 'Speaking Stones' (1998) also highlights the atrocities and massacres that have been a part of Indian history post independence. His other installations like, 'The Tools' (1993) and 'The Inner Voice' (1992), seek to bring out the intrinsic connection between religion and violence in contemporary India.

Seven Oceans and the Unnumbered Stars', on view at Bodhi Art, NY till October 27, 2007, comprises five sculptures and seven drawings. The artist is concerned with the question of 'being' and the creation of new meaning through displacement of objects. Both these preoccupations are contained within this current series of sculptures and drawings, although they are conceptually distinct from each other.

In 'Seven Oceans and the Unnumbered Stars', N, N. Rimzon views the body as a mere container - a receptacle of violence and of generative possibilities, simultaneous holder of secrets and emptiness. Using mythic beliefs of saint-poet Kabir and Buddha as a starting point, the artist has deliberately located his works in the present day, where every claim of faith and stated truth is subject to intense scrutiny.

There are traces of such apparent opposites in all his sculptures. In the relief 'Mother at the Shrine', the artist presents a roundel with a navel in the center; a pregnant belly full of possibilities but also a metaphor for the perishable clay pot that Kabir considered symbolic of the vulnerability of human life.

The sense of secrecy and the unknown inhabits the artist's drawings, emphasized by the omnipresence of enclosures and womb-like curved spaces. Although suggesting conventional 'realism', N. N. Rimzon however, has displaced the subjects from the space where they were originally observed; they are his 'intentional objects of sight'.

The absence of figures in his drawings communicates an oppressive silence expressing the human dichotomies of birth and death, life and destruction.

The intonation of these drawings, as in the sculptures, is reflective of the artist's distress with contemporary universal issues of violence and alienation. (Saafron Net, 2021)

From the Translator

The poetry collection is a translation of selected 21 poems from the poetry work of Dr Rajeevnath K. R.(Rajeev Puliyoor) based on imagery perception generated from the seminal works of N. N. Rimzon. The poet has changed sculptures and drawings of N. N. Rimzon into poems. The poetry works gives a taste on the works of both N. N. Rimzon and Dr. Rajeevnath (Rajeev Puliyoor). The poet Rajeev Puliyoor has given me the opportunity to translate his work into English which I graciously acknowledge.

Dr Harikrishnan M

PDF Scholar

Department of Education

University of Kerala

Incarnate Sources of Poetic Ideas

- **Rakesh Nath**

Modern Malayalam poetry enters a vast expanse that can only be seen when man ascends to the level of a visual text. The entry into the collection of poems, Seven Seas and Countless Stars, influences the reader to a level of energy called visual text, which should be further considered in terms of how patterns change a literary form of poetry. We have seen that some approaches follow a painting or a sculpture, revealing the limitations of language. But following this limitation of a collection of poems is a great miracle. Sri Rajeev Puliyoor Poetic Narration and Concept showcase a dialogue between life, the inner voice, the closed vessel. The struggles between them capture the poet in most of the poems. The approach that transcends poetry itself is evident in the visual mounting of the poem.

You should also try to look at the poetry as a sensory gland. Some metaphors that become materials in a sculpture have to be sought by a mouthpiece. I have to say that the idea that the reader of a poem should invent at least one metaphor has a lot to do with this work. All of these poems explore the potential of sculpture at a level where nature can be exploited. Digestion is a natural thing. But between the decay and a kind of substance of energy, some theories are expressed in the poem. But in language as a whole, Rajeev

Puliyoor uses the art direction of the art gallery. Rather than tribalism, the poet finds his poetic substance in the visceral pose, and we can see that the poet takes sculpture to the un relatedness between object and poetry.

According to Heidegger, not all linguistic archetypes on earth are psychological. Becoming such a carrier All these poems are travelogues. We can see such opposing elements and conditions in poems such as The Tree, Tools, and Consensus.

Earth A Sculpture

There is an attempt by all the poems to transform the earth into a canvas in such a way that it can be transformed into a sculpture. Some of the ways in which God and God can be transformed are manifested in the viewer and the reader. Just as it is done, so is coming and going in the nature of life. The language of the poem and the language of the subject matter are intertwined with something like Human - form - figures of a poem.

The smell of a flower when it blooms,

these are recovered.

I'm only thinking about this earth

in a deep rowing tonight

In my sleep

a mating dove has arrived.
In this westerly wind that leans
into the impersonal and subdues
the language of hysteria
Its Spring is just beginning

(Seven seas and uncountable stars)

Inner space

The stage and composition of music are closely linked to the literary form of poetry. Any art form has a large level to the inner space. In Western Poetry, the view that up-making is becoming a kind of traditional concept can be seen in new poetry magazines. Poetry has a special place in the field of Objective study if it is included as a fine - arts subject in possibilities such as the study of art of course. All these poems by Rajeev Puliyoor can be said to be moving poems. Poetry is a kind of movement that forms the core. To study it also means to make the object beautiful. Things like Michelle Foucault's question itself apply to poetry as well. Perspective and craft come second. The interior is described in sculptural art as a working space. K. G. Subramaniam's own, moving focus focuses on how to read space.

This collection of poems by Rajeev Puliyoor is significant for Indian Contemporary Poetry and Western Poetry Culture aims at a concrete stage in which the column type moves on to new basics (As used in poetry) A concept used in the form of theory to say that it existed not only in the new poems, but in all the old poem. Differentiation of Old and What is new Can be discarded here. Communicating ideology, in a way that defines the scope of writing, is both artistically and philosophically essential. Poetry needs to be seen as an art that changes situations. The language of poetry can also be seen as aimed at the working pace of sculpture. This kind of lyrical contribution by Rajeev Puliyoor is profound and evokes the Awareness of Art. An understanding of what the source of an identity evolves differently, where one poem becomes another and it becomes understandable. Rajeev Puliyoor's poems all, point to the way in which the sense of freedom in sculpture, in Indian sculpture, is transformed into an object.

From K G Subramaniam's 'wind' like works, molded to a stimulating exterior, Rajeev Puliyoor's visual text is a blessing, visible in Japanese myths, and leaves a distinctive re crafting at the roots of the poem.

Composition

Linguistically, poetry can be said to be a re-crafting of the visual form, measuring and influencing the space it determines.

Spiritual problems

Poems are tools that can actually be studied on certain levels of infinity. Sensationalism is the process by which poetry becomes a profession experiencing readers as great tools. Although it is not entirely possible to say that the center of poetry originates from the center of memory, the output of poetry is spread on spiritual reality. A kind of abstraction, an imperfect space, all of which makes it into such a reality, Poetry and symbolism, which occur when a poem enters a situation, create non-pervasive canvases.

There have been instances of a poetic scarecrow becoming a victim of expressionism in the Tamil Chola - Chera dynasty. It can be considered as an important part of Indian poetic culture. Such poetic studies as specific elements are apparently inhabited in modern times. The inability to find such position, even in the theoretical lore, significantly affects modern poetry and contemporary poetry because poets have to bear the burden of poetic reading. All of the collections of contemporary poetry that are being patched, however, do not affect some of the original movement of the reading. This cannot be changed into a view. This is because elements such as the natural Buddhism and Taoism of poetry seek Philosophy of poetry.

There have been some manufacturing defects of Poetics for Taoism and Buddhism. Only by being a sex story can we purify the poetic levels. Poetry has some dynamic connotations to the basic level of the material. Changes like design come to an art form and there has to be a psychological transformation from certain conditions of the Indian tradition. All aspects of this structurally affect creativity.What I personally follow throughout this collection of poetry is the way in which poetry is curated.

How to identify a poem

All the dimensions of a poem and its perceptions are aimed at certain references to the poem. The poets Neruda, Mayakavini, and Borges have all created a kind of unconventional poetic craft that should form the action of what is called poetry from references. We need to get back to the work of K G Subrahmaniam itself. The balance of energy has to be found here, both in poetry and in sculpture. Poetry is the composition of a reality. That is to say. The magnetism of poetry must be rooted in poetic culture. The average person needs to free him or herself from the effects of Indian heritage. Poetry's enjoyment is irrelevant. A poet arrives at an initial / finished work that restructures an image and convinces himself that he has written a poem.

The next step is to create poetry, and to create arguments about the sense of poets. "The Naturalistic Study of language, Chomsky Counters, has no place for a Platonistic notion of language, a notion of language outside the mind / brain is common to various speakers and to which each speaker stands in some cognitive relation. The reason is that this platonistic reification rests on notions like 'language' and 'community' that are hopelessly under -specified "

(Noam Chomsky- study by Norbert Honstein)

The intrusion of fake poetry

How true it is that Foucault said in 'Madness and Civilization' that a contradictory opinion is human instinct to the power struggles of defeat. There is an overflow in Malayalam poetry that makes it impossible to control thought in the contemporary context of poetry. While it can be accepted as a freedom, in linguistic terms it is language pollution itself. Another argument can be made about a private anarchy in language pollution itself. There have been many such studies on the desire for freedom. This can be seen extensively in Marxist studies.

Poetry and Socialism

The mystery lies in how Chomsky's linguistic space makes a people credible while passing through an inner conflict is also one of the main features. When it comes to the natural freedom of poetry, there are certain elements that are preserved as the divine gaining the spiritual psychology that seeks the cause of living. Elements of it may be - A Small Theory of Socialism. So an expression is not correct. But there is nothing wrong with saying an adjective.

I have to put forward another argument that poetry is a great irrational art. It is also worth noting here that this argument is one that seeks new literary heights from the super natural. It can be said that it is a traditional culture that makes every poet get blocked. It is an expression of whether poetry moves forward in the slightest (medium of poetry) in a way that recaptures reality, and the gas must also think about how a poet's relationship with his poem changes the composition, language, form, and rhythm of the poem. The poet's thought is something that is specially fused. Personally, I like to define poetry as an incomplete fusion of experience. There is a great deal of fusion between royalty / imagination in the medium of poetry. If we think of the medium of poetry at the level of process, each poet has a mind that goes beyond every imagery of poetry. The general sense of the poem, if not the general element, becomes apparent where the reader of the poem also has to adopt this course in poetic reading

Sensibility of Poetry

Poetry can be overcome by something like the harmony of poetry. Forget it. If the imagery can be turned into an in-depth event, the sensibility of the poem will increase. Poetry can also be seen as an emotion that is suppressed beyond the fact that it is only an inquiry. (Attribution to Foyd) Most poets are unable to increase the sensibility of poetry, and nimi tuta is such that the complexities of sensibility in folk art are lost in many majas. The poet is unable to use it, and the poem becomes a technique of assembling an eagle into other expressions and metaphors. It seems to extend to the personality of the poet. In fact, a great poet does not have to have a personality. Because poetry is closer to spirituality than the study of psychology, we need to examine the spirituality of the poet and the spirituality of the poem, rather than the spirituality of the poem itself. That is The sense of freedom in spirituality can be seen as a deliberate rejection of all spheres of a poem. The spirituality of the poet is born where the poet rejects his time, and as long as such a wind is blown in the poem, the poet will become a failed god. The totality of the poem is thus compounded by many influences. And that the poet himself becomes another great image. That is an interesting fact. When a poem is studied in a little more Zen-intellect and so on, it can be said which poet is which. What a poem.

Don't get me wrong P Kunhiraman Poetry is life in itself in. This similarity can be seen in all Western poets. The fact is that it is an experience, and that experience, too, is not a complete illusion, but one that has to be traversed and transcended.

What is poetry?

Understanding the state of poetry is recognized by transforming the very structures of the universe itself. Some earthly political thefts occur in a poem. The main problem is the material of the poem itself, where the poet succeeds in using poetry as a tool. Even the camera fails. The camera could not be conscious. Poetry makes it possible. We should consider it as the canvas of the body rather than the canvas of poetry. Writing a poem is a more meditative level than a spiritualist's. Canvas Thai tools can be used for sculpture and even storytelling. There are no poets in poetry. It can only be described as a hall, a back hole, where it is impossible to even enlighten the poet. The poet should seek the spiritual factory through poetry. The poet sees and maintains the body only as a tool.

The poet moves towards the fact that there is no depth. We should see all the movements of the poet only as a kind of spiritual analysis. (spiritual analysis) Some interventions of the period do not need to be grasped about the other 303 except to occasionally catch the path.

References

Moving Focus Essays on Indian (Art, 1978) Lalit Kala Akademi, New Delhi (Reissued by Seagull Books, Calcutta in 2006)

The Living Tradition, (1987) Seagull Books, Calcutta

The Creative Circuit.(1992) Seagull Books, Calcutta

The Life of Form in Indian Sculpture By Abhinav Publications Mr Carmel Berkson

Indian Sculpture 700-1800 Volume 2 of Indian Sculpture

Closed Vessel

Appear as Loneliness
 seated facing each other.
The pots seated together,
an idea inscribed.
Two voids or loneliness,
hands clasped and hugged together,
Like French kiss.

Inkling our fight with loneliness,
are conjugations,
in freedom less pleasant silence.
Morning blooms out red,
reddening pots more

expanding day's connotations.

Sky's Poetic erudition,
formed on wandering paths,
beneath all;
old age Sorrows,
even deeper,
taken aback,
a word 'I'.

Heaven's Home

Frightening Silence;
sword falls from chest,
  blood swiped by it.
  Frozen cold Surface,
  this Night.
sounds of a man,
walking via Altar.

Instruments

Words detached,
from domicile used.
A sound,
tete-a tete to ambit,
acts Sharp edges.
Earth after summersault,
darkness seen beyond,
still hidden weapon.
Word instrument,
evergreen silent sunlit,
trees animals vanish,
pugmark of tiger,

disturb meditation,
circular entity remains,
for all fall unto it.

Can instrument be moon,
whose instruments are stars?
there are instruments,
mopped up in silence.

After food,
what voidness remain,
in washed utensils.

Voidness of womb beyond birth,
a weapon forgotten to be taken.

The rust
where it lay,

wound on edge of clit,

blood of forest lay frozen.

Inside me lay fluttering,

incessant sounds of rusted weapons &tools,

realizing stationary start,

of rust coming by,

it scatters;

like bells falling unto silence,

rust a constructive mechanism,

A voids cover,

A draggers end;

A iron rods silence,

I babble.

Inside me,

Conclomations;
honey bee in
Core forest's darkness,
    I imagine rough surfaces,
    of centuries old Buddha statue,
    light, ascending on naked human body;
    some concepts, retrieved like ponds,
    shining swords from underwater,
    midday swallow blood.
Along ponds residing steps,
the skys above.
    Doors open like,
    bubble splashes in ponds,
    a man stands arms raised.

On The banks of Yamuna

Unidentified corpse;
broken pots brim lit with moon,
Night begins to fade away,
standing nowhere to go, I.
A befallen cry;
on its edge mother,
in her womb this star.
after being cutoff,
burned off the travel path,
vacuum after erase off,
meteors rays ring sky,
thinking of their origins.

Its repetition,
an ancient flow.

Non restorable damp dusk,
start and end of starry night.

Door's Nearby Temple

Door's nearby temple,
old ancient stars,
endless pathways.
    Doors staring sky,
    beneath spacious roofs,
    little darkness underneath;
    resembling keyholes,
    We dream;
    a night lonely and secure.
It come with us,
moon creating parallel,
ways through trees,

Night,

Darkness,

Staying;

Inner doors.

Where is it?

This Shelter;

walls laden with sweat,

made rough in cement.

Home beneath Moon

Tiles stacked above roof rafter,
silence of flapping wings,
flight unfinished,
sprinkled winter;
thickening representation.

Roof's tile end,
sound of falling dew drops,
doves in peak of sleep,
fall unto vague.

Melancholy paved house tops
hiding breath we lived;
dreams to peep moonlight,

a rope of stitched cloth.

    A sound uprooting trees from sky
    coming of wind;
    a dry summer night,
    crushing our voyage somewhere,
    a moment of joy;
    an odd summer rain in home,
    Our home beneath moon.

Like ancient joy,
Like ancient sorrow,
we went asleep,
after washing utensils,
on roof tops branches,
withered and dead by hug,

like crackling finger joints,
falling down from sleep,
above moonlight,
Night lay remnant,
fingers of night touch moon,
fingers smear in moonlight.

Two trees;
Kiss,
each other,
their fingers touch each other,
in the winds.

Stains oozing out from,
cupids dart of night flowers,
lay smeared in moon,

Kisses;
Creating,
Safe grips.
    Trees
    around home,
    bowing in dawn,
    blooming by day,
    bow to sun,
    by dusk,
    evening prayers,
    etched in,
    symbols of day.
Frozen by night
search liberation,

kindness in roots,

nest were birds sat and vanished,

Voids.

    An ascending breeze came by,

    many blows,

    in rough branches.

Depth of black,

nights mark,

remain;

moon unvarnished,

fallen unto sky.

    Roof of home,

    bowed branches,

    home beneath moon.

School nearby Church

School near church,
way around playground,
A walk,
Reaching the chapel again;
Kept like heartbeat.

Intervals, we look unto,
Chapel see church walls,
Bell rings scattering,
Sow sorrow into us,
when none walks by,

way touching the church,
shadows of men,
going unto solitude,
and light of morgue mingle,
where they left by.

Lined cemetery's,
cold cement,
summer unburned,
Like circling love,
Like wine kept to pour,
earth's conclomation.

A wind holding by,
lazy to come by,
stand were even dry leaves stand still,
school verandah we left,
in outer verandah,
our silence start commotion,
in its cycle we leave again.

Church alone
into interior it stand,
time commutes into it,
a lonely pray,
encircling a everlasting silence,
begin again to construct.

On the sloppy roofs,
midday laden itself,
bell rings in between sleeps,
courtyard's vacant from holidays,
from cross seen above tiles,
time limitlessly flow;
Its crawling scar.

Home near Pond

Houses never cease,

unquenched thirst;

In liitle wave wings,

goes into day dreams depth;

blooms like earth's woven youth,

Kissing wave less times.

Ways zig zag,

walked in washed legs,

come back unto me;

branches vanishing with tender leaves,

in forthcoming cold wind,
Jack's consciousness in watery steep,
Reclaims depth.

Bound together are two ways,
going around home,
on walk down verandah,
darkness melts away,
branches overlooking blue water,
in blues,
pleasant silence bathe,
mirroring evening prayers.

Big immersions untouched,
lay unfathomed gorges,
home laid wind ridden,
depth overturned;
a zenith tower.

Rainy season;
vanish into imagery.

Death of forest

Houses roof,
signs of wetness,
trees hugged by branches;
darkness where silence lay,
a night drawn in charcoal,
trees cut down,
The drawing;
below sky devoid of stars.
    Before forest death,
    a wood cutter;
    wander in light for loot,

star's in dreams,
hearing music play,
time tickles away,
sharpening blade's stay,
seeing deep forest,
in dreams embrace,
branches redden in kisses.

Rain pour down,
in exaltation of night flower,
night cuts open to;
loose darkness.

In deep forest boundary,
memoirs of forest curves.

From rest on this day,

reclined axe wiped again.

Beginning to scatter,
opening sky's colours,
Streets;
lay in its boundary,
The forest.

Last Visitor

Night;

lantern's extinguished,

in silent intervals of bell rings,

Last visitor.

Pot's Under the Tree

Branches stand,
handshaking each other,
knots not unfurled,
movement of blood ,
Shared each other.

    Forest;
    observed in night,
    appear, day yet to come
    face to face.

Drought become drawings,
words said,

branches seated together;

in them;

are spaces,

crumbling crushing

Silence.

Returning to deep forest,

under trees,

two pots.

Sky littered by stars,

Silence;

lighted itself.

Trees

I wish;
a dhyana,
in branches tickling trees.

In vanished love of trees,
tender leaves resurrect,
I remain to believe,
days are wetted day light.

In meditation's moonlight,
ability to,
see marshes drowning,
ability to see,
love and sun wetted.

Broken branch;
unlike marsh,
for my return and vanish.

Unlike love,
I am its end.

HOME

Will dusk of yester years,
still be there even now.
Dusk kissing slopes,
unseen by deep tree roots,
herd of goats,
The hill;
sky seen
climbing uphill,
what next?
time dug,
walked grounds,
grass cut,

bushes;
a bundle of chaff,
memoirs of destroyed trees.
Looking aback at void left,
voidness of chaff and stable,
voidness of pond covered.
Pondering;
Wavy trees tinted in sun,
hovering leaves,
shadows move to and fro,
After years,
search for same days.
A home in holes.
A home in void.

TEMPLE NEAR BLUE POND

Cold breeze always need come by
broken bell rings from sky,
mirrored on surface,
depth retrieved,
the seconds;
It begins to come by;
becomes philosophy.
    Dug into depth,
    fighting blows of height,
    bird's lane,
    nude sky walkers,
    clouds and hundred million stars

lay overturned.

Pond, a carved blue statue,
sculpted before temple,
swim an unfinished work,
night dense with stars and trees,
searching meditation in immersed water,
fishes on surfaces,
stars with depth,
Go for ancient travelling.

Temple stand paralleling both,
a sculpture carved stone,
a sculpture dug stone,
In depth,
sit frozen in past;

A stone

scratches of unfinished work,

lay in it,

un ended songs of silence,

chisel sticked;

love scrolls.

    Sacred water sprouting,

    In secret lips.

SILENCE OF FLUTE

Burned out

fallen;

This second!

A song came by.

Fingers drawn

over hair,

trees stand,

like nerves travelling inward,

like blood coming through spaces,

fingers drawn in air,

forgotten travel on earth.

Hands shaken away,

thought of villainy silence,
singer immersed in own song,
travelling through woods.

Forest non forgetful
cyclic chain,
core of fallen tree,
like strengthening prevalent silence,
silence flute's core,
flower's reincarnate,
forming void of mind,
bird's returned several years after,
enter same den,
leaven forest's sorrows,
searching in darkness.

A tomb

like widow’s open home.

    Rain lashing on top,

    light’s burning silence,

    music lay,

    between trees,

    a verse less song,

    meaning grasped silence to,

    touch fire.

Flute’s hole

wind lay solo,

that’s it;

Silence!

NIGHT'S POND

Night,
thick foliage sleeps,
pond's unconscious motion,
laying sideways in a dream.
    Coconut trees bounty,
    falls asleep,
    lost grip,
    Pondering Stars scattered in water.
Moonlight roamed slowly
left earth far behind,
Into slopes of sleep,
got lost in infinity,
circumventing branches.

MAN AND TREE

In your silent solitude shores
an untied boat,
stay lonely,
loneliness without flow,
a flower in thought of
deserts dreadfulness,
regained they,
blossoming smell,
regained like prayers.

This flow,
flow ended.

Clasped hands,
might look upon,
shredding leaves.

Life,
branches from tender barks,
resurrecting hands,
singing old odyssey,
reincarnating leaves,
dried love nuts,

new life yet to come,
roars in subdued waves,
began etching,
taken aback,
memoirs of tree depth,
there wood pieces lay,
summer lay dry.

CAVE TEMPLE

Swords rust's return,

in bend scabbard,

Jailed wind makes noise,

scrubbing solitude,

Rock temple,

the rock itself;

revealing century old tales,

petty counts,

mark of the fallen.

HUT'S UNDER TREES

'Poduvanni' tree,
slant's upon roof,
'Manjapavitta' flew kisses,
a thousand butterflies,
on its branches.

'Poovam' stands straddled,
frozen and rooted!
letting no passer's by,
'Pottakavalam' seeds,
Broken smell swept beyond hills,

Snake trails!
Snake trails!

Tree roots broken,
go diving deep,
a way circumventing tree;
while another bending away,
when evening lights lit,
in gate house darkness usher,
evening prayers reach gateway;
to return.

Night crawls upon,
ways, huts and trees,
dawn's spreading upon valley,
like rolling downhill,
with voids left,
by palm parrots,

headless coconut trees
stand guard.

unknown ways wind flew,
dog ditching head hooked on plate;
our memoirs stacked,
like collapsing stones,

The water oozing,
from the voids,
create monsoon.

Summer came as rain went,
beneath same trees,
our huts,
we lay unto sleep.

EVENING BEACH

Evening;
skies scattered boundaries,
come closer day dwindle off,
a girl sitting between rocks,
look into sea,
assures dusk's withdrawal,
unto sea,
sit listening clasps of waves,
surfs on rock smeared,
generate night's thirst,
in girl,
fallen rocks imagery.

Earth and sky

Stars withering away,
one old night,
dew drops stuck on brim,
shaken away by breeze.

Night, a deep rowing,
thinking of earth alone, I
a dove who lost partner,
come into my dreams,
in bed,
one who sweat all day,

stars of night ,
wither away fall.

My consciousness
a bird broken who fathomed,
unconscious ocean,
weak, peep me from windows.

www.ingramcontent.com/pod-product-compliance
Lightning Source LLC
Chambersburg PA
CBHW062113160726
48282CB00026B/782
9789354732799